BORDER TERRIER

INTERPET
PUBLISHING

The breed

The Border Terrier was finally acknowledged as a distinct breed in the late 1800s. The breed was named in honour of the Northumberland Border Hunt. Northumberland is in the rugged border country between England and Scotland, which with its rolling heather-covered heath land, is well known for its rough terrain and bleak aspect. The Border Terrier was recognized by the British Kennel Club in 1920.

Borders were originally developed by local shepherds and farmers to control the fox population. Foxes were a particular problem in the border country, as the livestock was mostly left to range freely. Later, Border Terriers were used in formal fox hunting, where they were used to flush foxes from their lairs. This had a great influence on how the breed was developed. Border Terriers were expected to be fit and agile enough to follow a horse, wiry enough to burrow underground, and calm enough to fit in with a pack of excited foxhounds.

Although today's Border Terriers remain rugged-looking and hardy, their tough exterior belies a sweet nature and an excellent character. These dogs can make wonderful pets and companions and are becoming increasingly popular.

Published by
Interpet Publishing,
Vincent Lane, Dorking,
Surrey, RH4 3YX, UK.
Tel: 01306 873822

©2014 Interpet Publishing. All rights reserved

ISBN 9781842862445

Printed and bound in China

The information and recommendations in this book are given without any guarantees on behalf of the author and publisher, who disclaim any liability with the use of this material.

Contents

1 INTRODUCING BORDER TERRIERS

The Border Terrier is a small, medium-boned sturdy little dog that does not have the manicured, sculptured look of the other terrier breeds. His shoulders and body are narrow, and his front legs are straight but not too heavy. His tail is medium-sized and tapers from the base. His distinguishing feature is his otter-shaped head which, combined with a moderately broad skull, dark hazel eyes (which are quite widely spaced) and a strong muzzle, with a black nose, makes him one of the most appealing of terriers. A dark muzzle is desirable for show dogs. Borders usually have quite a serious expression and have strong teeth with a scissor bite. Border ears are usually v-shaped, set on the side of the head, and drop forward close to the cheeks.
Borders usually have a rough double coat. This is short, dense, and wiry and is comes in several colours including red, grizzle and tan, blue and tan, or wheaten. They may also have a small amount of white fur on the chest. This is essential for a working dog and it is easily maintained.

Most Borders are wonderfully healthy, active, and very affectionate dogs who respond very positively to love and attention. They also get on well with children, other dogs, and animals. Their training should be started early, and the intelligent Border is usually very easy to train.

ORIGINS

The Border Terrier did not become an official breed until the middle of the 19th century. The breed name comes from its long association with the Border Hunt in Northumberland. Borders share their ancestry with the Bedlington Terrier and the Dandie Dinmont Terrier. The

three breeds all originate from the Border region and are distantly related. The breed was first recognised by Britain's Kennel Club in 1920.

THE BORDER TERRIER CHARACTER

Border Terriers are working terriers, bred to hunt, to chase and kill. They can be described as being a big dog in a small dog's body and are excellent house dogs. But they are not aggressive with people and are not yappy. Indeed, the Border is an ideal first dog, especially for families with children.

Border Terriers don't like to be left on their own for too long and really like the company of other dogs. This love of company is one of the reasons why border terriers fit so well into a family environment.

A very intelligent and dignified

SINGING DOGS

Most groups of Borders will howl or sing several times a day, for just a few seconds or a minute at most. Even tiny puppies in the nest will sing. This charming characteristic was probably acquired from many generations living with Foxhounds in hunting kennels, who are also known for their vocals. Border lovers describe their singing as an angel choir, but it may not be so popular with the neighbours. Single Borders tend not to sing. Musical owners report that their Border likes to join in with their music making.

breed, Borders are very responsive to training. They always seek to anticipate their trainer's commands and try to do what you require without being told. To tell off your Border you will only need a raised voice as they are extremely sensitive dogs, and have been known to ignore their owner for several hours, or even days, after having received a telling off, until they feel forgiving. Border Terriers are affectionate and mild-mannered and will always be trying to please you so they really dislike hard words.

Borders are also

ABOVE: *You will have a wider choice of puppy if you decide to have a male, as it seems that there are more male puppies born than bitch puppies.*

brave and will rarely show that they are in pain. Puppies being taken for their vaccinations never make a fuss or cry. This makes them very popular with vets. Borders are usually a very clean breed and don't take very long to house-train. They also travel very well in the car and few Borders are travel sick.

Borders integrate well with other animals and many live in harmony with cats, chickens, sheep, cattle, horses, and ponies. But Borders are hunters and should not be trusted with other pets such as hamsters, guinea pigs, rabbits, and birds.

Borders are a very playful breed. Border puppies and adolescents are very active and seem to retain their youthfulness into old age. They love to play with toys and learn all kinds of games and tricks. They are also well adapted to competitive obedience and mini-agility. Several Borders have excelled in these fields and compete at the highest levels. As terriers, they also like to dig and it would be a good idea to install reinforcements along the bottom of fences.

Borders were bred to hunt and have a lot of vitality and stamina and are very active and energetic dogs. Once they are fully grown, they need plenty of exercise and enjoy a long walk. But Borders don't need to need an active lifestyle every day, and are quite happy to relax and play at home if you don't have time to take them for a long walk. However, Borders can be quite greedy, so it's very important to adjust

ABOVE: *Borders possess a harsh double coat – essential for a working dog and easily maintained.*

their calorie intake to their level of exercise. Too much food and too little exercise can easily lead to your Border becoming obese.

A Border's wiry coat needs to be brushed and kept clean but they do not tend to pick up much dirt. Borders have slightly longer legs than many other terriers, so their tummies usually stay clear. The breed colours also seem to shrug off the dirt, unlike white-coated breeds. Border Terriers need hand-stripping (plucking) to keep their coats tidy at least a couple of times a year. One of the benefits of this is that you do not get shedding around the home. If you are unable to do it yourself, there are many professional groomers who can do this for you.

Borders were bred to hunt and have a lot of vitality and stamina and are very active and energetic dogs. Once they are fully grown, they need plenty of exercise and enjoy a long walk. But Borders don't need to need an active lifestyle every day, and are quite happy to relax and play at home if you don't have time to take them for a long walk. However, Borders can be quite greedy, so it's very important to adjust their calorie intake to their level of exercise. Too much food and too little exercise can easily lead to your Border becoming obese.

A Border's wiry coat needs to be brushed and kept clean but they do

COLOURS

The blue and tan colour has become more popular in recent years for the show ring, possibly because this colour of coat is very easy to keep tidy, enabling owners to keep showing the dogs even though they may not be in the best of coats. A small patch of white on the forechest is quite normal and, occasionally, puppies have white tips on their toes which usually disappear when they get older.

ABOVE: *All Borders are active and game but bitches may be a little more independent by nature.*

ABOVE: *Border boys are loving and warm and like to keep close to their owners. This example has a grizzle coat.*

not tend to pick up much dirt. Borders have slightly longer legs than many other terriers, so their tummies usually stay clear. The breed colours also seem to shrug off the dirt, unlike white-coated breeds. Border Terriers need hand-stripping (plucking) to keep their coats tidy at least a couple of times a year. One of the benefits of this is that you do not get shedding around the home. If you are unable to do it yourself, professional groomers can do this for you.

FINDING YOUR DOG

Once you have decided to get a Border Terrier, you need to find a highly regarded breeder. One of the best ways to do this is to contact a Border Terrier breed clubs. Clubs often have lists of litters that have been bred by their members. If you can, it is highly desirable to meet the breeder before you decide to buy. A good breeder will want to know that you can offer a good home to one of their puppies and you can see the conditions in which your pup has been bred. Another good way of contacting breeders is to visit dog shows where there is a Border Terrier. This would also give a wonderful opportunity of meeting some Border Terriers close up and seeing the different sexes, sizes, and colours of Border Terrier. The UK Kennel Club also has the Assured Breeder scheme where their members can offer litters on-line through their website. This is an excellent way of buying a dog for showing if that is your ambition. But maybe the very best way to find your puppy is by personal recommendation from someone who has already bought a puppy from a breeder of Border Terriers.

MALE OR FEMALE

Many potential Border Terrier owners say that they would prefer to buy a bitch puppy. This is

Naturally, if you are looking for a Border Terrier as a loving pet and companion, you need to look for a puppy from an affectionate and healthy environment. In the past, Border Terriers were often bought as working dogs, and were trained to catch rats and rabbits. These animals were often specially bred for this purpose. Of course, any Border may hunt instinctively and some are even specially trained to hunt rabbits with the help of trained ferrets.

Alternatively, if you want your Border Terrier to be a show dog, you should try to source your puppy from a successful kennel. Breeders who sell budding show puppies will be well-placed to advise you about the potential of their puppies and give you an idea of how they will develop. A show puppy should appear balanced and attractive, and carry himself well. But buying a show puppy is always tricky. A puppy that looks like he has loads of potential at eight weeks of age may have faded by the time he attends his first dog show at six months. The most difficult thing to predict is how his adult teeth will come through, as correct dentition is so crucial to a show dog.

As we have described there are several classic Border colours. But it is far more important to find a dog that you will love rather than pursuing a dog of your preferred colour.

because they have heard that Border Terrier dogs have a tendency to wander and that they don't have such good temperaments. In fact, this is completely wrong. Male Borders are actually very unlikely to roam, while bitches are far more likely to have an independent streak and leave the safe confines of home. In fact, many devotees of the breed think that dogs make the best pets. They have good characters, are very trainable, and don't suffer the reproductive health problems that bitches are prone to: they don't come into season every few months, and don't have false pregnancies. For these reasons, trainers usually prefer dogs for obedience training and mini-agility competitions. It is true however; that bitches are sometimes more relaxed than dogs. But it is certainly worth considering a dog as a pet. Dogs may also be better hunters if you want your Border to keep down pests.

2 CARING FOR YOUR PUPPY

You need to make some important preparations before your collect your puppy and bring him home. You need to decide where you want your puppy to sleep, eat and exercise and which parts of your house you will allow the puppy to go.

Consistent behaviour on your part will help your puppy feel secure and settle down quickly, so start as you mean to go on. All dogs need to have a routine and it is best to get this established as soon as possible.

PREPARATIONS

Before you collect your puppy you must make sure that his new environment is free of any hidden

ABOVE: *The big day arrives when your puppy must leave his littermates and travel to his new home.*

ABOVE: *Puppies enjoy playing in the garden.*

hazards. Very importantly, your garden needs to be well fenced. A puppy needs only a tiny hole to squeeze through. Any openwork gates should have wire mesh attached, and any dangerous garden equipment should be put away. Indoors, you must make sure that electrical cables and phone wires are concealed.

Its also a good idea to put away anything you really don't want to be chewed. You really don't want to be telling off your new puppy on his first day in his new home.

SLEEPING ARRANGEMENTS

One of the most important things to decide is where your puppy is going to sleep. This is crucial as this is somewhere that your puppy needs to feel completely safe and secure. It

DOG CRATES

A dog crate is usually a collapsible plastic or metal enclosed pen that is just large enough for a dog to stand up and turn around in. The crate is a place for the dog to be when no one is around to supervise him. It is the dog's bed and sanctuary. Its purpose is to provide confinement for reasons of safety, security for the dog, housetraining, prevention of destructive behavior, and/or travel. If you use the crate correctly, it can have many advantages for you and your dog. You can enjoy peace of mind when you are out, and your dog can feel safe and secure. Your dog can also travel safely in the crate.

RIGHT: *You will need to decide where your dog will sleep, eat and exercise and where he will be allowed to go in the home.*

your puppy won't be able to get into trouble in the night. A playpen would be ideal for this. The floor of the pen could also be covered with newspaper. Although there are many different kinds of dog beds on the market, the simple plastic kidney-shaped baskets, which come in many different sizes and colours, are some of the most practical. They resist chewing and can be washed and disinfected. They can also be filled with cosy pads or mattresses on which the puppy can sleep comfortably. These mattress inserts can usually be washed in the washing machine. It's a good idea to buy two of these in case of accidents! An excellent idea is to replace the fabric softener in the washing cycle with a slug of disinfectant to make sure that any germs or bad smells are destroyed. Wicker baskets can be dangerous when chewed as the sharp sticks can damage the puppy's mouth or throat. Equally, bean bag beds can easily be chewed through and the polystyrene beans they contain are difficult to clean up.

should be a place that suits you both you and the dog. The most important thing is that the sleeping area should be warm, dry, and completely draught free. Many owners prefer their new puppies to sleep in the kitchen or utility room as these rooms usually have washable floors. But you should not let him sleep in a confined space where there is a boiler in case of carbon monoxide leaks. You could also fence off a small area so that

ABOVE: *A bean bag is one option or there are plastic beds which are more resistant to chewing.*

COLLECTING YOUR PUPPY

The best age to collect your puppy is when they are around eight weeks old. When you arrange a time to pick him up from the breeder, a time around mid-morning is often the most convenient. This will give the puppy a good chance to feel at home by bedtime. He will be able to sniff around his new home, be cuddled by his new owners, eat, play, and sleep before he faces the night alone.

If you plan to collect your puppy by car, it is a very good idea to take someone with you. That means that one of you can drive safely and the other one can comfort the puppy. A bottle of water for a longer journey might also be useful if the puppy gets thirsty. If you have to collect the puppy on your own, it is important that you ensure that you will be able to drive home without distraction. A loose puppy could jump about and might cause an accident, so you will really need to equip yourself with an enclosed basket or cage to contain the puppy safely. A snugly blanket would also be nice. You can then put the basket or cage on the passenger seat,

ABOVE: *Give your puppy a chance to explore his new home – and to meet all the members of his new family.*

17

ABOVE: *It is important to arrange insurance for your new puppy as soon as possible*

where the puppy can see you. You can secure the basket by pulling the seat belt across to hold it firmly. It might be a good idea to take a towel and some newspaper in the car in case the puppy is travel sick. Puppy trainer pads are a new product that can also prevent accidents from staining the car seats. They can also be very useful when you take your puppy for its vaccinations.

PEDIGREE AND RECEIPT

If you buy a pedigree Border Terrier from a breeder, they should give you a signed copy of your new puppy's pedigree, showing his forebears for several generations. As well as being very interesting, this will almost certainly be needed if you want to register your dog with your national Kennel Club. This will be essential if you want to show your dog or breed pedigree puppies. Your puppy's breeder will also need to supply you with a signed receipt for your new dog. This should specify your dog's details, the sale price, and any special arrangements, guarantees, or declared faults that the puppy has.

INSURANCE

It is very important that you arrange pet insurance as quickly as possible.

Many breeders sell puppies with a month's free insurance arranged through one of the major pet insurers. This normally covers your puppy for death, veterinary fees, and third party liability. As vets fees become increasingly expensive, pet insurance gives many dog owners a lot of reassurance.

BELOW: *Your puppy will be a bundle of energy.*

19

ABOVE: *Make sure family pets meet the new puppy under supervision at first.*

No-one wants to end up with a large and unexpected vet's bill for vital treatment. There are an increasing number of insurers offering pet insurance. Many insurers offer whole life cover for your dog. This is where the insurer continues to insure your pet even if they have an on-going health problem. Although these policies may be more expensive, they ensure that you won't be left without cover

in an emergency. Third party liability insurance is also very important. If your dog were to cause an accident or damage you could end up being liable. This is sometimes covered by household insurance policies, but not always.

ARRIVING HOME

Bringing your puppy home is a very exciting time, but you should try and keep the atmosphere as quiet and calm as possible. Let your puppy explore his new home, and show him his bed. You should also take him outside to show him where you would like him to relieve himself. Puppies need to go to the toilet at least every couple of hours. Young children should be shown how to stroke the puppy very gently and you should explain that they should not disturb him if he goes to his basket for some peace and quiet. You also need to remember that your puppy is unprotected against illness until he

ABOVE: *Do not change your puppy's diet until he has had a chance to settle.*

ABOVE: *Do not allow your children to touch the puppy when he is asleep in his bed; this is his space and, when he is in it, he should be given peace and quiet.*

has had all of his vaccinations, so it would be preferable to keep visitors to a minimum during this time. Outsiders may unintentionally carry infections into your home.

Give your puppy a small meal when you get home, but remember that he may well not feel up to eating for a while. He may feel a little intimidated by his new surroundings and may miss his brothers and sisters. It is quite normal for a puppy to have a brief loss of appetite but this should be short-lived. Your puppy may well want to sleep shortly after you arrive home,

exhausted by all the new sights and smells. Puppies need a lot of rest at this early age.

THE FIRST 24 HOURS

Although your brave Border puppy may not cry when you leave him alone to sleep, he will almost certainly miss the companionable warmth of his litter mates. A warm hot water bottle wrapped in a towel or blanket may help, and a puppy-sized cuddly toy for him to snuggle up to may also cheer him up. A ticking clock wrapped in a blanket may also soothe him until he is settled.

LEFT: *A soft cuddly toy can help the puppy settle down to sleep.*

Although it is very tempting, beware of going to your puppy if he cries during his first night with you. This is giving him the message that you will come running whenever he cries. If you go to him, you may also be tempted to take a miserable puppy into your own bed, but you should think about this very carefully before you do. Once you have allowed your dog to sleep with you, they won't ever want to go back to sleeping alone. Is that what you really want? Even if they aren't very happy at first, brave Border puppies often don't make a sound. But even if he does cry, the chances are that the puppy will soon settle down and fall asleep from sheer exhaustion. Once he has got through one night on his own, he will soon settle down to his new routine.

FEEDING

Any good breeder will provide the new puppy owner with a diet sheet with details of the feeding regime that your dog has been used to. Many will also give you enough food for a few days until you have a chance to get some yourself. Its best to stick to the breeder's diet for a while at least as the puppy's stomach is delicate and can be upset by an abrupt change in its feeding routine. The breeder should also let you know when the puppy was wormed (and when he needs to be wormed again), and give you details of any vaccinations that the puppy has had. You should ask for a vet's certificate for these so that you and your vet will know exactly what protection the puppy still needs.

BOWLS

You will need at least two bowls for the puppy, one for food and one for water. These need to be shallow sided so that the puppy can reach his food and water easily. Food can also be served on a saucer when the puppy is small. As he grows, you will need to replace these puppy bowls with larger, deeper sided bowls. Heavy stone ceramic dishes are hygienic and won't get knocked over, even if the puppy is searching for the last morsels of food. Stainless steel bowls are also clean and unbreakable, but they are light and easy to push around and your puppy may even try to chew the edge. Plastic bowls are far too easy to chew and drag around, and won't last five minutes. Swallowing pieces of plastic is also potentially dangerous for your puppy, as they can form sharp edges.

ABOVE: *He will need to settle with you before having lots of strangers visit.*

COLLARS

When you collect your Border puppy he will only be around eight weeks old, and he will still be very small. Even a special puppy collar shouldn't really be used for such a young dog.

In fact, a collar will only be necessary when your puppy can go into public places after he has his full course of protective vaccinations. Your puppy should be exercised in his own garden until that time. If you want to put a collar on your puppy, you should use a

ABOVE: *Soft puppy collars*

ABOVE: *Your puppy will need a water bowl and a heavy pottery bowl is less likely to tip.*

RIGHT: *Shallow feeding bowls are easier for your puppy to eat from.*

very light and soft one, but you should be careful that this doesn't get caught on anything as this will scare the puppy and may make him nervous of the collar.

TOYS
There are many kinds of dog toys on the market, and all puppies love to play. However, you need to make a very careful choice of which toys your puppy is allowed to play with by himself, as many can present a hazard. Strong-jawed Borders are quite destructive when they chew their toys, and an adult can remove the squeaker from a squeaky toy in a few minutes flat. Solid rubber balls last much better, and many Borders like to play fetch.

Although rawhide chews, which are available in many different shapes and sizes, are very popular, they can also be dangerous and puppies should not be allowed to play with them unsupervised. Specifically, chewed-off pieces of hide can present a choking hazard. The larger hard-pressed rawhide chews may be harder to destroy and but puppies should not be allowed to have these by themselves.

Dogs of all ages like to chew and this is particularly important for puppies so that they can teethe. Chewing encourages the baby teeth to come out and the adult teeth to come through. Deep-fried knuckle bones will keep your dog busy for ages. Even in

ABOVE: ABOVE: *A knotted rope makes a good plaything.*

warm weather, these bones keep for a couple of weeks. Most dogs love them, and once the fatty bits have been chewed off, they don't make a mess. Soft knotted ropes are also good for chewing and for games of tug-of-war. They may also help to keep your puppy's teeth clean. The worst dog chew is an old shoe or slipper. This will almost inevitably lead to the destruction of your good shoes at some point.

ABOVE: *Another puppy is the best plaything!*

HOUSE TRAINING

House training is the first sort of training that you should begin with your puppy. It should begin as soon as you first arrive home with him. With vigilance and positive training methods, most puppies quickly learn how to be clean in the house. House training will be easier if your puppy has a settled routine, sleeping and eating at the same times during the day. Puppies usually need to relieve themselves when they wake up, during play, and after meals. You should also watch for signs indicating that your puppy wants to go to the toilet; restlessness, whining, tail raising, sniffing, and circling around. You should take your puppy to the same place in the garden on each of these occasions. You should encourage him with a consistent phrase such as "toilet." As soon as the puppy performs, you should praise him and play with him.

A puppy should never be chastised for making "mistakes." Instead, you should say a firm "no" to the puppy and take him outside to his toilet area. You then need to clean up as well as possible so that no smell lingers. This might give the puppy the idea that he can use that spot for his "business" in the future. While some puppies are easier to house train than others, you should remember that your puppy will not have full bladder control until he is about four months old.

ABOVE: *Toys are important for puppies to chew on - particularly when they are teething.*

25

ABOVE: *You must keep your puppy at home until he is covered by vacinations for diseases.*

VACCINATIONS

Puppies need to have their first vaccinations between six and nine weeks and a second set between nine and twelve weeks old. In the UK dogs are routinely vaccinated against five potentially fatal illnesses: distemper, hepatitis, parvovirus, leptospirosis, and kennel cough. Parvovirus is particularly deadly, as it attack's the dog's major organs. Dogs should then be given a booster vaccination each year to maintain their protection. Your breeder may have started the course of injections, in which case you need to know exactly what your new puppy has had. Most injections are given into the ruff at the back of the dog's neck,

but kennel cough vaccine is given as drops into the dog's nose. You may also consider having your puppy micro-chipped at the same time. Micro-chipping will become compulsory in some parts of the United Kingdom in the next few years.

It might be worth postponing your dog's vaccinations if the puppy appears unwell. It is quite common for dogs to appear a little unwell after his vaccinations, but if this persists for more than a day, you should take him back to the vet.

Your vet will advise when it will be

ABOVE: *You can train your dog to use a dog harness which fits into the seatbelt catch. This is useful for small cars.*

GROOMING

Wire-haired dogs like Border Terriers make great pets if you're house proud – because they don't shed their coat. But they still need dog grooming and attention to keep them in tip top condition. A metal-toothed comb and a stiff-brittle brush will help you de-tangle your adult dog's coat. But your puppy's much softer fur will require a much softer brush. Brushing your puppy will help get him used to the grooming process. The breed's thick paw pads mean that their claws often don't wear down naturally and will need clipping with a pair of special canine nail-clippers. Nail-clipping should also be started in pup hood.

stiff-bristled brush

metal-toothed comb

nail-clippers

medium-bristled brush

safe for your dog to go out in public, and to mix with other dogs. This will be when he has developed full immunity.

Your Border will need a rabies vaccination if you want to take him abroad. You will also need to treat your dog against the tapeworm Echinococcus multilocularis one to five days before you bring him back to the UK. Tapeworms are a common parasite that are found in the small intestine of dogs and can grow up to 20 centimetres in length.

3 GENERAL CARE

Feeding a good, wholesome diet to your Border is central to his healthy development and growth. It will also give him the best chance of a long and happy life with you. The competition in the dog food market means you have a huge choice of food for your dog.

The new complete dog foods offer a balanced and nutritious feeding solution for your dog, but you need to choose which diet would be best for your dog and which will be the most suitable for his wellbeing. There are a range of options.

DIET

Over recent years, there has been a tendency to feed pet dogs with a complete diet of specially formulated dry dog food. Dry dog food is available at many different price levels. These diets don't need anything adding to them and can be fed either wet or dry. They include all the vitamins and minerals that you Border needs. In either case it is very important to make sure that your dog always has access to clean, fresh drinking water as dried food can make your dog very thirsty. Dried foods are usually supplied as either small pellets or balls and are available in various different nutritional balances for dogs of different ages and sizes. Of course they are also very

clean and easy to use. The fact that they keep well means that there is almost no waste food. Pasta-type dry dog foods are also available. These need to be soaked and include dried meaty chunks and gravy.

Even if you also offer your dog a mixed diet of meat and biscuits, a certain portion of your Border's diet should always consist of dry food as chewing will help to keep his teeth clean and healthy.

Some Border owners prefer to feed their dog a variety of home-cooked meals. These should include raw or (usually) cooked meat, vegetables, carbohydrates, as well as vitamin and mineral supplements.

If you decide that you would prefer to feed your Border with home-cooked meat, you can buy frozen mince at pet shops. This comes in various flavours including beef, chicken, and rabbit. This meat is suitable to be fed either

ABOVE: *Deep-fried knuckle bones are very good when puppies are changing their teeth.*

29

ABOVE: *Make sure your Border is supervised if there is food in reach*

raw or cooked and can be prepared in the microwave to save time. Cooked tripe is also popular with many dogs. The meat or tripe can then be mixed with a medium bite-size wholemeal biscuits. You should ensure that these biscuits are good quality. They all have different additives and ingredients and some are definitely better superior to others. Some of the biscuits can be moistened, but some should also be left dry. Although this method of feeding your dog takes more time and trouble on your part, many dogs really enjoy this kind of diet. However, you should consider adding extra vitamin supplements and may wish to discuss this with your vet or an experienced Border breeder.

A very wide range of canned and foil-sealed dog meats are also available. Canned dog food has been very popular for a number of years and is fairly convenient. Although some of these meaty foods are marketed as being complete, they can also be added to biscuits. This is probably better for their teeth. Some manufacturers offer their own biscuits to add to their canned or foil-packed food. One thing that is important with these nutritionally-dense foods is the quantity offered. You should follow the manufacturer's advice pretty closely and make sure that you know the actual weight of your Border so that you can be as accurate as possible. Canned and foil-wrapped foods come at all prices and some are inevitably better than others. Some of the cheaper brands of canned food contain a lot of jelly or gravy.

QUANTITIES

As Border Terriers tend to love their food, it is particularly important that you keep an eye on the number of calories they consume each day. Your dog needs enough energy to be bright and active, but not enough to put on excess weight. You should keep an eye on the amount of food your dog eats each day and include any treats or table tidbits that he is given in your assessment, as well as his main meal. If you notice that your Border is putting on weight, you should cut down his food a little or move to a low calorie alternative. It's much better to do this as soon as possible rather than let a serious problem build up. As your Border ages, this is particularly important.

FEEDING HAZARDS

Some Borders do have a tendency to be greedy and for this reason it is very important that they are not given large pieces of meat or food. If a dog tries to swallow a large piece of food whole, he can choke and even die, especially if he is alone at the time. Borders also have a tendency to scavenge and so you should make sure that food is not left around that could also cause him to choke.

EXERCISE

Exercise is an important part of keeping your Border fit and well. This should begin in puppyhood. You will need to build up a routine of daily exercise gradually, as puppies can be damaged by being over-exercised. The best thing is to let your puppy play outside in good weather, in a securely fenced area. It is better not to train the puppy on the lead until they are at least fourteen weeks old, and then for just a few minutes each day. Puppies shouldn't go out on the lead until they are around five months old and then just for a short walk. As they develop, their walks can become longer as they gradually become acclimatized to strangers and traffic. This way the puppy will gradually cope with the new experiences he will face in his adult life. As yours dog's bones and joints become stronger they can go for a ten or fifteen minute walk a couple of times ago in addition to having free play time in the garden. Exercise is also very important for the mental health of

BONES

You should be very careful before you give your Border any kind of bone. The safest are probably deep-fried knuckle bones, but even these should not be given when the dog is unsupervised. Borders can rub off some of their facial hair with excessive chewing, so you need to make sure that he isn't chewing for hours at a time.

31

your Border, by avoiding boredom. A good exercise regime will also help your dog to be calm and relaxed at home. A consistent amount of exercise helps to avoid injuries.

HEALTH CHECKS

In order to take good care of your Border, it is important to recognise any health problems as soon as possible. It is very helpful to set aside some time each week to check over your dog from nose to tail. If problems are noticed early, they are much easier to treat. Prevention is always better than cure. Your routine grooming is probably the best time to check that all is as it should be.

ABOVE: *Adult dogs will appreciate a brisk, daily walk.*

TEETH AND GUMS

A Border Terrier will usually get his adult teeth at around the age of four-and-a-half months. You need to check which puppy teeth are loose and which have fallen out, and to see how the new ones are coming on. Gently lift the lips to check the teeth. Be especially careful if your puppy is teething. It is good to get your Border used to this procedure so that both you and your vet will be able to examine his mouth without too much trouble. You should check the tongue to make sure that it looks normal, and check the dog's teeth and gums. The teeth should be clean and free from tartar. If tartar builds up on the teeth his

ABOVE: *Un-vaccinated young puppies should only play in the garden.*

TOOTHBRUSH

To clean your dogs' teeth you need a special dog's toothbrush or a clean piece of soft gauze to wrap around your finger. You can get special canine toothpaste from your vet or use a paste of baking soda and water. Don't use fluoride with dogs under six months of age as this can interfere with their enamel formation, or human toothpaste, which can irritate a dog's stomach.

LEFT: *Accustom your puppy to being handled gradually.*

breath will smell, the teeth will become discoloured and eventually the gums will be affected, leading to infection.

EYES

You need to check your dog's eyes regularly as eye problems can be indicative of other health problems. You should watch out for excessive crustiness, tearing, red or white eyelid linings, tear-stained fur, closed eyes, cloudiness, a visible third eyelid, or unequal pupil size. Border Terriers are prone to weep a little and this can be diminished by keeping your dog's hair away from his eyes by plucking this away. Removing this will also prevent the hair under his eyes from becoming stained. If you see any other eye symptoms, contact your vet immediately.

EARS

You can also use the weekly check to keep an eye on your dog's ears. If your Border's coat gets too long, this can cause ear infections. The hair growing thickly around the ear and this prevents air circulating. If your dog is scratching, shaking his head and holding an ear slightly away from the head, this might mean that your dog has got ear trouble and you need to consult your vet. You can also buy special ear cleaners that help to clear excessive ear wax.

NAILS

Your Border's toenails should also be checked regularly. This includes his dewclaws if they have not been removed from the newly-born pup. Most breeders remove dewclaws to prevent them becoming a problem. Dewclaws on the hind legs are virtually unknown in Borders, although these do appear on dogs of other breeds. Remaining dewclaws can become a

CLIPPING NAILS

Unless your Border spends a lot of time walking on hard surfaces that will help to keep his claws short, they will need regular clipping. If you hear them clicking on a hard

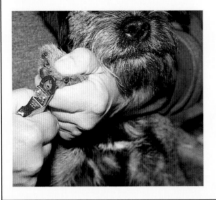

surface, it's time for a trim. Most dogs dislike having their feet handled, so getting your dog used to this ritual at an early stage helps you both weather the process. A dog's claw is made up of the nail itself and the quick, which provides the blood supply to the nail. Avoid cutting into the quick because it will bleeds profusely and it is very sensitive. Don't worry if you can't do all your dog's nails at once, you can clip them one paw at a time, with other activities in between.

LEFT: *Nails need to be trimmed on a regular basis unless your dog walks on roads routinely.*

problem because they are not in a position to be worn down and will occasionally grow in a circle, or grow so long that they can be a nuisance to both dog and owner, as they can scratch your hand or arms very badly when you play with your dog. They can also be caught and become very sore.

In fact Borders do not tend to wear down any of their nails, so they need to have their claws trimmed on a regular basis. If the nails are allowed to grow long, the quick inside the nail also grows longer. The quick is the pink line in white nails; it is not visible in black nails. If this happens it means that the dog's nails cannot be trimmed back properly and, eventually, the foot will become out of shape and may become uncomfortable.

THE BORDER COAT

One of the most identifiable characteristics of the Border Terrier is his coat. A Border in good coat should not look too groomed and smart. As a working terrier, a Border Terrier has a naturally hard, wiry outer coat and a dense, short undercoat. A working Border wears off dead hairs on bushes and rocks but retains enough of both coats to protect himself from bad weather and the damp. So a proper Border coat is of medium length. It doesn't look too shaggy but neither is it stripped to the undercoat. When grooming, the aim should also be to achieve a natural appearance, not a sculpted one. While many of the other terriers are clipped, chalked, back-combed, and super-groomed, a

ABOVE: *The border coat is harsh and dense compared to other terrier breeds.*

Border should always look as natural as possible.

As important as the coat is the Border's pelt, hide, or skin under his coat. A show judge should feel both the Border's coat and his pelt to evaluate him properly. The Border's breed standard is the only terrier standard that requires a loose-fitting and thick hide. This thick hide enables the Border Terrier to work his way in and out of narrow openings when he goes underground in pursuit of his quarry. It also protects the dog from scratches and bites. A correct hide is critical to Border Terriers, and a gentle pinch is not sufficient to assess it. Both hands should be able to grasp the hide on a Border's back and raise it slightly.

Border Terriers come in a great range of colours. They may be red, grizzle and tan, blue and tan, or wheaten. Border reds range from a rich, foxy red to shades of light or coppery red. Grizzle refers to the dark tipped hairs which give an overlay of colour to a red or tan coat. Blue and tans and dark grizzles are distinguished by the undercoat. A blue and tan Border will have a black undercoat. Rare wheaten Borders are a clear light tan. When they are born, most Border puppies are dark and, except for blue and tans, it is difficult to predict the colour of the dog's adult coat. They nearly all have a ring of coarse silver hair about a third of the way from the base of the tail, and most have dark ears and muzzles.

The major task in grooming your Border Terrier is to pull out, or strip

HAND STRIPPING YOUR BORDER TERRIER

1 *Chalk makes the hair easier to grip.*

2 *Take off a few hairs at a time.*

3 *The hair comes out quite easily.*

4 *The undercoat is a different colour.*

The finished result.

its old coat when it has "blown." This means that some of the outer coat has become overgrown and dead. At this point the hair can be pulled without any discomfort to your dog. We are describing the general procedure of how to do this but you will soon discover which particular combination of methods and grooming positions work best.

First, place your Border on a non-slip surface at a convenient working height and choose your grooming position. Most people prefer to strip out the coat standing behind the dog, others prefer to face the dog. Many people also think that stripping certain areas of the coat (for example, the hair on the back legs) is easiest with the dog lying on its side.

If you are standing at the back of your dog, use one of your hands to grasp the dog's hide at the shoulder firmly enough so that his hide will not move when you pull on the hair. With your other hand, pinch a few hairs between the thumb and index finger and pull them out with a firm and quick motion. Make absolutely sure that you are doing this in the direction that the coat is growing. Strip the dead hairs evenly from the coat, making sure to keep the hide from moving in each area you strip. If you are standing at the front of your dog, steady him with one hand and use the thumb and index finger of your grooming hand to pull out the hairs in quick pulls working in

ABOVE: *If you have to bath your Border before a show, do so at least two weeks before the day*

the direction that the coat is growing. Many Border Terrier owners find that a block or pot of chalk helps them to get a better grip on the dead hairs. Others choose to use a stripping knife. This is also used to improve your grip on the hairs you are stripping out. It acts as an extension of the fingers. To use a stripping knife, trap a small number of hairs between the thumb and the underside of the knife and pull the hairs out, working parallel to the coat and close to your dog's body. Make sure that you are pulling in the direction that the coat is growing and be sure not to cut into the coat.

BATHING

Generally, Borders do not require frequent bathing. Towelling off when wet and dirty followed by a brushing when dry usually suffices. Bathing also tends to soften the harsh coat that is naturally dirt repellent. If a Border gets dusty, a rubdown with a damp towel works well. Borders do not normally have strong odour. However, it is wise to bath your Border after the bi-annual stripping procedure to soothe his skin, especially if your dog's skin is particularly sensitive. Some Border's skin can go very red after stripping and these dogs may need bathing two or three times with dog shampoo to calm the skin down.

Do not be tempted to bath your Border Terrier before a show; as this will make your dog's coat soft and fluffy. As the Border is a wire-haired breed, this is not what the breed standard calls. If you really need to bath your Border before a show, try to do this at least two weeks before the day; as this will give the coat time to settle and the natural oils time to return.

Clipping is not recommended for Borders as this does not remove the

dead hair but merely shortens it. It will also lose the texture and colour of his natural protective coat. If a dog's coat is clipped in error, it can be restored with two or three hand strippings. For their comfort some older Borders are maintained by clipping.

THE VETERAN BORDER TERRIER

To many people their veteran Border Terrier becomes more precious as he ages. He will have given you the best years of his life to be your companion. There are still some lovely times that you can have together. Border Terriers can live to a good age. Thirteen to sixteen years is typical and Borders have been known to achieve even greater ages.

As you dog ages, his needs will change and you will need to tailor your care of him to accommodate this. Dogs over ten should be taken for shorter walks at his own pace. Of course, each dog will age at his own rate, so you need to keep his general wellbeing under constant review. Your older dog's dietary needs will also change. Not only will he will no longer require as much food, but his teeth may not be as good as they were. It might also suit your older dog to eat two smaller meals each day so that his digestive system can cope better. There are several special diets on the market for the older dog which may be appropriate for your older Border.

Your older Border should be always

ABOVE: *The Border Terrier may live to 13 or 16 years of age.*

kept comfortable and warm and you shouldn't him to get cold and wet. Make sure his bed is somewhere warm and free of draughts. He will sleep longer, and more soundly than when he was younger. Many Border Terriers go deaf in old age, so you should be gentle when you approach him, especially if you need to wake him up.

If you have younger dogs, make sure that your older Border isn't left out of the fun, but don't allow your younger dogs to annoy your oldie, disturb him when he is sleeping, or let your younger dog knock into him.

It is even more important to keep your mature Border Terrier well groomed and trimmed. This will not only help his wellbeing and ensure that, if there any external lumps or bumps appear you will see these quickly. If you notice any changes of this time, be sure to take him to your vet as quickly as possible.

Ultimately, if your older Border becomes to fail in his health and is losing his quality of life, your vet may recommend that you consider putting him to sleep. Although this is a terribly sad decision for the loving owner to make, you owe it to your loyal Border to prevent any unnecessary suffering and the loss of his dignity. The modest little fellow in brown will have done everything you have asked of him, and deserves this final kindness from you.

39

4 TRAINING

Pups enjoy learning new tricks and skills. Early training allows owners to capitalise on their pet's receptive and confident young mind. If your puppy came from a good home, he will be used to being handled. This is very important and you should make sure that you get him used to being groomed; having his nails clipped, teeth cleaned, and ears checked and cleaned. This will prevent a lot of heartache later on. Small puppies are usually very compliant and will soon get used to this treatment. This handling will become invaluable if you decide to show your dog.

TRAINING YOUR BORDER PUPPY

Although Border Terriers are usually very affectionate and intelligent, they can also be quite stubborn dogs. Because of this, it is a good idea to start your dog's training as soon as possible. There are also a couple of bad Border habits that you will need to discourage.

Many Borders tend to nip as people pass, and may even do this as a form of endearment. You need to discourage this with a firm "No!" at the puppy's eye-level or by clapping your hands together. As soon as the nipping behaviour has stopped, and you dog

ABOVE: *If your dog is used to handling it will make it easier if you decide to show your dog.*

has calmed down, you should reward him with a gentle cuddle. Remember that this nipping could be quite scary and dangerous from an adult dog and needs to be discouraged. Any Growling should also be discouraged.

Borders also have a tendency to run around indoors and hide under the furniture. This is just an exuberance of energy and a facet of their natural desire to dig. This needs to be channelled into safe outdoor play. It is also a good idea to establish an area where your Border is allowed to express his need to dig!

LEARNING THE BASIC COMMANDS

You also need to teach your puppy some basic commands and encourage him to follow them. The puppy will respond best to a regime of positive affirmation rather than by shouting and smacks. This harsh regime doesn't work and will damage the trust between you and your Border. Because your Border craves positive attention from you, all your training should be by encouragement and rewards. Eye contact is particularly important. Your puppy will try his best to understand what you want but remember that a puppy's attention span is quite short, so a few minutes training mixed in with play is the best way to go.

If your puppy makes a mistake a firm "No!" in a deep voice should stop him in his tracks. Borders will try to please all the time but a few mistakes

are inevitable. Although you should always be kind and gentle to your dog, you do need him to regard you as the "top dog" and respect your wishes so that you can live together very happily.

One of the most important rules that you should observe is to be as consistent with your dog as possible. Don't allow him to do something one day that you are going to tell him off for on the next. For example, don't allow your puppy to sit on the armchairs if you don't want him to do this in the future. This will help your commands to be clear to the puppy, and he will understand the way you want him to behave much more quickly. Consistency will also help your dog to trust and respect you, which is the foundation of the future relationship that you will enjoy together over the years to come.

COMING WHEN CALLED

Start to teach your puppy his name as soon as you get him and use it all the time, especially at meal times and

ABOVE: *Give a treat when the puppy responds to a command.*

when you give him a treat. Train him to come to you by calling his name and rewarding him when he comes to you with a cuddle or treat. This will soon become second nature to him. Coming when called is important for your dog's future safety and for your peace of mind so imprint it into his mind at an early age. Remember that your dog will be much faster than you when he grows up, and he will be able to run away, making it difficult for you to catch him. A good idea is to carry a treat in a crinkly paper bag. If your puppy doesn't come on command, you can rustle the bag while you repeat the command. As soon as he has made the connection between rustling paper and the treat, he will always come to you. When he does, you should stroke and praise him.

If your Border decides to disobey you, use your growly voice to get his attention. Once you have it, you should immediately change your tone to a soft and encouraging tone and call him again. This should do the trick. When he has obeyed you, give him a treat and praise him. You should also remember that however angry your dog has made you by refusing to come when he has been called, you must never punish him when does finally comes to you. This will confuse him completely and undermine his trust in your leadership.

LEAD TRAINING
Most Borders very quickly learn how to walk on the lead. Their natural inclination is to keep close to your heel so attaching a lead rarely causes a problem. Twelve to fourteen weeks is a good age for a puppy to start wearing

his first collar. The puppy's neck will be very soft and delicate so you should use a very soft and comfortable collar. Your puppy will soon grow out of this puppy collar, so wait until he is at least six months of age before you buy an expensive collar.

The best place to begin training your puppy is in your garden. In this safe and controlled environment, your puppy can learn about walking on the lead where there is nothing to upset or distract him. Encourage him and praise him as he walks well, but do not allow him to rush forwards and pull. If he does, keep calm and talk to him, then persuade him to walk a few steps, then praise again. It will not take long for him to learn. Calm lead work will build a strong bond of trust between you so that when he meets new things he will look to you for reassurance.

SIT

All Borders should be taught to sit, whether or not you intend to show your dog. An easy method is to hold your hand over your dog's head, holding a reward. Inevitably, your dog will look up at the treat. Use your other hand to very gently push the dog's behind into a sitting position, while saying "Sit!" in a clear, firm tone. As soon as he sits, give him the treat and praise him. Gradually move away from pushing his behind so that he will sit for the reward, then just for the command and praise.

STAND

You will also need to teach your Border to stand or "stack" if you want to show him. Stacking is when the dog stands squarely and still. Traditionally, Border Terriers are shown free-standing, assuming the correct position following commands from his owner. "Hand stacked" dogs have each leg put in position manually while the handler stands or kneels very close to their dog.

To teach your puppy how to stand free you need to practice so that he will stand correctly for a reasonable length of time. This can be done with treats, by gradually increasing the time has to stand correctly to get his reward.

If you just can't get your dog to stand freely, you can teach him to be hand stacked. Start with the "Sit"" command and then gently put his legs into the desired position. You should do this kind of training little and often so that your dog doesn't get bored.

ABOVE: *The Down is taught with the aid of a tidbit.*

THE DOWN

The Down is a very useful command that can diffuse a difficult situation if, for example, your dog is jumping up. First, ask your dog to sit in front of you. Once your puppy is in the Sit position, take a treat into your hand. Lower the treat slowly to the floor so that your dog's nose is between their paws. Now give the command "Down." As soon as their elbows touch the floor, praise him and give him the treat. If you repeat this exercise several times, your puppy will ultimately respond without having to give him a treat. If the puppy will not go down, you can give very gentle pressure on the forequarters to encourage him to go down to the floor.

STAY

Learning to "Stay" is a great way of getting your dog to exercise some self control. Ask your dog to sit and give him calm praise and a small treat. Keep treating the dog as you move around him. We are teaching him to stay sitting whatever we are doing. When

he has done enough, give him a release command and reward him. The next time, try the same technique but with praise rather than treats. Finally go back to him and give him a treat. If you want to add distractions try dropping a treat or a toy in front of your dog. Hold him back from picking this up. As soon as he relaxes, praise him and give him the release command. This exercise will take time and patience; little and often is best as the puppy will become bored with it. It may be helpful if you use a hand signal as well as the command "Stay", which will help the puppy understand.

ABOVE: *The Stay exercise should be built up gradually.*

NOISE

Now that noise pollution is such an issue and the cause of so much ill-feeling between neighbours, it is good to know that Borders do not bark or yap without good cause. They will bark when there is a disturbance, or someone comes to the door, but they are a generally quiet breed. Young dogs in particular may also occasionally bark and howl when they are left alone at night. You need to go in to him quite promptly to assert your authority and tell the dog to be quiet. Do not take him back upstairs with you!

The one noise that Border Terriers do tend to indulge in is "singing." There are lots of videos on YouTube showing Borders singing along to various popular tunes. This habit seems to go back to their early heritage when they lived along with hounds. Most Border Terrier owners do not find this offensive but I am sure there are many people who would and do. Only Borders don't seem to sing very often, but two Borders will usually sing for around thirty seconds several times a day. They will usually stop when you ask, but you should be aware of this, especially if you have close neighbours.

TRAINING CLASSES

Another point of view can often be useful if you feel that your Border's training isn't going very well, or if you feel it has reached a plateau. You need to look for a class that

ABOVE: *Borders are so intelligent that they really enjoy being stretched by advanced training.*

you and your Border will enjoy, run by an experienced dog trainer that uses modern methods of positive reinforcement. Formal training can also give you a new perspective on your dog's abilities. Classes can also be a good place for your puppy to learn to socialize with other dogs, and for you to meet other like-minded owners who have their dog's welfare at heart. The best way to find a good training class is by recommendation, but you can also find good classes on-line. Local breed clubs will often have connections to local trainers. You may decide that you only want to go to basic obedience classes, or you may decide

ABOVE: *Mini-agility is popular with Borders.*

that you and your dog could benefit from learning more advanced levels of obedience. This might also lead to competing in Obedience Competitions.

There are also specialized Ringcraft classes that are specially designed for Border owners that want to show their dog. Ringcraft classes can be very

ABOVE: *Jumping through hoops is fun!.*

sociable, as everyone attending them will have a strong interest in their dogs and a desire to show them. Ringcraft classes are offered at several different levels, from dogs that are still in their puppyhood to experienced dogs who just want to brush up on their technique. Ringcraft training is quite intense and it greatly enhances the bond between dog and owner. Most Ringcraft veterans will tell you that the most important thing for show success is that your dog enjoys the classes and wants to be a show dog.

MINI-AGILITY

Mini-Agility competitions for dogs have become very popular in recent years. They were first introduced into the UK in 1978. Agility tests your dog's fitness and the handler's ability to train and direct the dog over various obstacles. Border Terriers have done really well in Mini-Agility and many people now buy Borders with

Mini-Agility competitions in mind. Several Borders have qualified for top competitions.

Mini-Agility is for the fit and active dog and owner. It is fast, furious and a great favourite with competitors and spectators. A high degree of trust and training is required if you wish to compete, although many owners do it just for the fun of it, with no intention of becoming competitive.

ABOVE: *Border Terriers can befriend livestock.*

THERAPY DOGS

Border Terriers make fantastic therapy dogs and many Border Terriers are registered as Pets as Therapy, or "Pat Dogs." Under this scheme, dogs can visit patients in hospitals and residents in homes for the elderly. This brings comfort to those who can no longer keep a dog, or those who miss their own dogs while in hospital. It has proved to be a great success and, as the Border Terrier has such a kind and extrovert temperament, they are ideally suited to this work.

THE GOOD CITIZEN SCHEME

This scheme was introduced by The Kennel Club in 1982 and is the largest dog-training programme in the UK. The aim is to encourage owners to train and socialize their dogs so that they become a joy to the community. Open to all dogs, the scheme is non-competitive and the emphasis is placed on the standard of achievement.

LIVESTOCK

Although Border Terriers were originally bred in the countryside, they are highly adaptable dogs and can live very happily in both the town and country. Border Terriers that live in rural areas should be taught have to behave around livestock, including sheep, cattle, and horses. This should be done from an early age. Your training should have established that you are in charge and so, when you meet this kind of livestock, you will be able to stop your puppy from worrying them. If you live in the country you should introduce your puppy to this kind of temptation. Town-dwelling Border owners should be aware of the livestock hazard when they go out into the countryside. You should always keep your dog on a lead near livestock or wild animals.

Clicker training

Clicker training for dogs started in the 1960s, but it has become increasingly popular over the last few years. As an intelligent breed, this kind of positive reinforcement training is particularly suitable for Border Terriers. If you use the "click and reward" technique, it is possible to train your dog to engage in all kinds of games with you, and you can also use a clicker for more general training. Dogs of any age, from puppies to veterans, can enjoy clicker training.

Essentially, the dog trainer uses the clicker to signal to the dog that his behaviour is good, and that he will receive a treat. The trainer needs to be careful that a treat is given for each click. If you break the association, your dog will soon lose interest. The treats need to be very small. Something soft that the dog can eat quickly works best. This could be thinly sliced sausage, small pieces of cheese, or tiny training treats.

For clicker training to be effective, it is essential that the click is well timed on each occasion. In other words, the click needs to coincide exactly with the behaviour that you want (sitting, for example). The click is a signal to your Border that he is doing what you want, and that you are going to reward him. Teaching the dog to watch your face, so that he is concentrating on your instructions is an excellent first step in clicker training. You can gradually reinforce this training so that you can still get your dog's attention in very distracting situations, where other dogs and people are around.

There are two ways in which you can add the clicker to your training regime. In the first instance, you decide what you want to train your dog to do. If this is lying down, wait until you see your dog lying down, then click and treat. Keep doing this until the dog lies down when he hears the clicker. You can also reinforce the clicker training with verbal commands.

The other way to use the clicker is to gently move your dog into the position you want (lying or sitting, for example). Once the dog is in the position you want, you click and reward him to reinforce this behavior. If you do this several times, the dog will come to understand what your commands mean. A "cue" is an alternative to a verbal command. For example, you could tap the ground if you want your dog to lie down. As soon as he goes down, you then click and reward. If you find that you are having problems communicating with your dog, it may be that you are clicking too late, and not reinforcing the behavior you want clearly enough.

To teach your dog more complicated tasks, you may need to break down the assignment into a string of shorter steps before re-combining them.

Clicker training can also be used to train your dog out of bad behaviour. For example, if you don't want your dog to bark each time someone comes to the door; you can click and reward him for being quiet whenever there is a knock or a ring. If he barks, stop clicking and rewarding him.

One thing that you should always bear in mind is that clicker training is a bonding exercise between you and your dog and mistakes should never be punished. It is sufficient that mistakes are not rewarded with a click and a treat. You should keep as calm and positive as possible during your clicker training sessions. If you feel that your dog's attention is wandering, or you are beginning to feel frustrated, you should probably give up for today.

BRAIN TRAINING

Brain training is another popular form of modern dog training. The idea behind it is that many of our canine companions are bored and intellectually under-stimulated in their everyday lives. Brain training is a method of teaching your dog new games and bonding with him at the same time.

One great game that your dog may enjoy is the vocabulary game. Starting with your Border's two favourite toys, teach him to fetch each one by name. You can reward him with a treat, or a click and treat. If he gets it wrong, keep repeating your request and gently guide him to the correct toy if necessary. You will be able to use this technique to very gradually build up his vocabulary until your Border knows the names of several toys, and can bring them to you on command. This is tough brain work for your dog, so you should reward him each time he brings the correct toy. Super brainy canines have been able to build a vocabulary of more than two-hundred words this way.

The benefits of extending your dog's training can be immense. Your stimulated dog is happier and better behaved. This interaction between you will also serve to deepen your mutual understanding, and your bond with each other.

CLICKER TRAINING TIPS

- A good tip that might improve your clicker timing is to think of your clicker as a camera. You snap the clicker to take a picture of the good behaviour you want, not the behaviour immediately before or after this.

- If your dog hates the sound of the clicker, try to deaden the sound with a cloth or a piece of cotton wool. When he comes to associate the click with a treat, he will probably forget his reservations about the noise.

5 SHOWING YOUR BORDER TERRIER

Many Border owners decide to show their pet as a hobby. It's best to get some highly qualified advice as to whether your dog is of show quality. The best person to offer this advice might be the breeder from whom you bought your dog. Alternatively, you could go to a Club show and ask for an unbiased opinion about your dog from one of the senior officers of the Club.

SHOW TRAINING

Border Terriers are so flexible and intelligent, that they can start their show training as both young puppies and as slightly older dogs. Your dog's basic obedience training and general socialisation will prove to have been a very good investment whenever your dog's show training begins.

One of the first things to get your Border puppy to do is to stand freely. As the breed is judged as the dogs stand on a table. Your dog also needs to be calm about being handled so that the judge can examine his paws, tail, genitalia, and ears. Practicing this is very helpful. A table with a non-slip surface is helpful so that you can move the dog a standing show position. You probably need to do this every

day until your dog is completely at ease. Once you have established this, you will only need to go through this exercise from time to time.

Ringcraft is the other important thing for you and your dog to learn. This includes lead training for the show ring. You need to teach your dog to walk on a loose lead at your side, on both your right and left hand sides. It is most common to show your dog on the left side, but occasionally judges will ask for a manoeuvre which will mean he will have to walk on your right side. Your dog must not pull on the lead.

You will also need to teach your Border to stand or "stack" in the show ring. Stacking means that the dog is standing squarely and still. Traditionally, Border Terriers are shown free-standing, assuming the correct position following commands from his owner. "Hand stacked" dogs have each leg put in position manually while the handler stands or kneels very close to their dog.

If you just can't get your dog to stand freely, you can teach him to be hand stacked. Start with the "Sit"" command and then gently put his legs

ABOVE: *Show training can start when your puppy is young.*

into the desired position. You should do this kind of training little and often so that your dog doesn't get bored.

SHOW EQUIPMENT

You won't need a lot of equipment to show your Border. All you will need is a light slip lead or show lead, a metal-toothed comb or a pin pad, (this is useful for giving your dog a last-minute groom). You also need a ring clip to hold your number. If you decide to progress to Championship Show level you will need slightly more equipment, such as either a wire cage or travelling crate in which to keep your dog safe or a chain to secure your dog to his

bench, a blanket for him to rest on, water, and a drinking bowl. If the show is a long distance from home, you will also need to take some food with you.

PRESENTATION

Presentation is crucial to doing well at dog shows. Of course, one of the most important aspects of show presentation is your Border Terrier's coat. This needs to be in a clean and tidy condition. Borders should not be bathed just before a show. This softens the coat and goes against the breed standard, which calls for a harsh coat for this traditionally working dog. Ideally you should strip your Border's

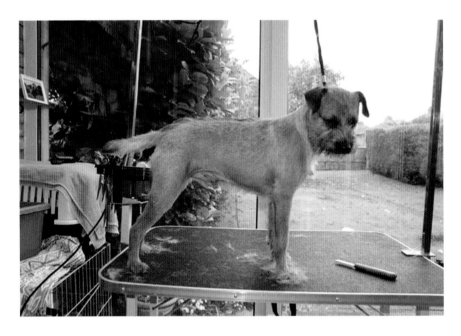

coat eight to twelve weeks prior to his first show. This will give him a new coat all over, which will be looking its best. Your dog should also be the correct weight for his size and in a fit condition. About a week before the show, trim any stray hairs around the paws and trim your dog's nails. Don't forget your own appearance!

Naturally, you should wear clean and tidy clothes, but you should dress simply so that you don't detract attention from your dog. You should also wear flat, comfortable shoes as you will be on your feet for several hours and need to be secure on your feet to lead your dog in the ring.

ENTERING A SHOW

Most dog shows ask their participants to fill in a set of entry forms. You need to fill in these show entry forms very carefully, as mistakes may mean disqualification. In the UK, your dog also needs to be Kennel Club-registered in your name before you can show him. Novice owners may think that if a dog has been registered by the breeder, he can be shown. But this is not the case. Make sure that you arrive at the show in good time so that you and your Border can settle down in the busy atmosphere and relax.

IN THE RING

All dog show judges have their own system of judging, but most judges will ask participants to line up as a class. The judge will then ask you all to move together before inspecting the dogs individually. They will then ask you to move your dog on his own so that he can give him a full inspection. Most judges start their examination at the dog's head. This will include looking at your Border's mouth to see if he has the breed's correct scissor bite. The judge will feel the body, forequarters and hindquarters. He will also check your dog's paws, pads and his tail. The judge, with both hands, will span the dog behind the shoulders and lift him briefly to assess his weight.

The judge will then ask you to move the dog around the ring. He might ask you to move up and down, or in a triangle. This is so that he can assess

LEFT: *The show dog's coat requires a lot of attention.*

BELOW: *The judge will examine each exhibit in turn.*

53

the dog's movement from the front and rear and in profile. When the judge has reached a decision, he will place the dogs in order of merit. Don't take it too badly if you don't win on this occasion, you and your Border may be more lucky next time you venture into the show ring. Judges' opinions on dogs can differ widely so, at another show with a different judge, you may get a completely different placing. But the most important thing is that you Border is most of all your pet and companion, and nobody else's opinion of his merits should have any bearing on that.

A GUIDE TO THE BREED STANDARD

Most Border owners are interested in comparing their dog to the breed standard. Of course, if you want to enter your dog into shows this is even more important. Since the breed was first formalized in the early years of the twentieth century, Border breeders have closely guarded the breed's characteristics. Borders are essentially working terriers and should look as though they are capable of doing the job they were bred for. The Border's origins are reflected in the breed standard. These are terse and to the point and closely reflect the

ABOVE: *The Breed Standard calls for a game, active dog with the appearance of a working terrier.*

qualities that are required for a dog that is expected to go to ground after a fox. Border's need a powerful pair of jaws, good bone but not heavy, and a chest that is not too wide for him to get out of any earth he enters. A Border also needs to have the stamina to keep up with a horse, in order that he will be there when he's needed. He is basically a worker, but is has the perfect temperament to be an active member of a family, combining good nature with a terrier's gameness

One of the most identifiable aspects of a Border's appearance is its head and so it's not surprising that the part of the Breed Standard which refers to the head is perhaps one of its most important statements. A Border without the classic otter head will never show successfully. The head symbolises the breed. The skull is broad with a short strong muzzle, and a black nose is preferable, although a liver or a flesh-coloured one is allowed.

ABOVE: *A Border's upper teeth should closely overlap the jaw. This is known as a scissor bite.*

Your Border's eyes should be dark, not prominent, not round, not too close together, but not too wide apart and have a keen expression. His ears should be small and 'V'-shaped, of a moderate thickness, and dropping forward close to the cheek. They should not be too high or close together as this would give the dog a Fox Terrier-like expression. His ears should not stick out sideways or 'fly.'

The mouth should have a scissor bite, with the upper teeth closely overlapping the the jaw.

RIGHT: *The Border's otter-shaped head is the symbol of the breed.*

ABOVE: *The skull is broad with a short strong muzzle, and a black nose is preferable.*

The Border's neck should be of a moderate length. Not so short that the dog appears to have no neck or too long and swan-like. The neck should also be well set on, merging gradually with strong withers, forming a pleasing transition into the top-line. The neck should not have an upper, arched portion of the neck.

The forelegs should be straight and not to heavy. They should not be too wide apart or close together either, and not be too heavy in the bone.

A Border's body should be deep, narrow, and fairly long. The ribs should

BELOW: *A red Border Terrier.*

ABOVE: *The Border Terrier's temperament is calm which makes it a good show dog.*

be carried well back, but not over-sprung. It should be possible to span the dog with both hands behind the shoulder. The dog should not be large in the rib. This is so that the dog should be able to go to ground, and return to the surface after completing his work. The dog's loins (the part of the body between the final ribs and the hindquarters) should be sprung, and strong. The underline is gradual, not cut up like a whippet.

The ideal Border hindquarters should be racy, i.e. they give an impression of speed without loss of substance. They are long from hip to hock, short from hock to foot, and have a good bend of stifle without exaggeration. The feet should be small and tight, not open, spread or flat, and have thick pads capable of standing up

to a day's work.

The tail should be moderately short, fairly thick at the base, then tapering. It should be set high, and carried gaily. It should not be curled over at the back. It should never be docked. The coat is the dense, harsh, thick coat of a working terrier and Borders are coloured red, wheaten, grizzle and tan, or blue and tan. Ideally, dogs should weigh between 6kg and 7kg (13lbs to 15.5lbs) and bitches should weigh between 5kg and 6kg (11.5lbs to 14lbs).

Preserving the characteristics of the Border Terrier means that these dogs have stayed close to their hardy roots. This hardy breed was selectively bred to be extremely brave and tough and make feisty pets and fantastic companions in both town and country.

6 BREEDING

Breeding a litter of puppies can be very rewarding, but you should remember that it can also be a costly and time consuming experience. But each pregnancy will put your bitch at risk, so you need to consider the pros and cons very carefully.

RESPONSIBILITIES

It would be wise to get expert advice before you decide to breed a litter from your Border Terrier. You should not breed from your bitch if she has any health issues or faults that she would perpetuate in her puppies. If you have little or no experience of dog breeding it is a big commitment to breed a litter. You will want to make every effort to ensure that the puppies that you breed have sound temperaments, are healthy, and are good examples of the Border breed. You will also want to make absolutely sure that your puppies go to good homes.

Before you go ahead and breed your litter, you would be well advised to ask yourself some serious questions. Do you have the time to look after your litter until they go to their new homes (around eight weeks)? Are you knowledgeable enough to advise your puppies new owners about the various aspects of caring their puppies,

including their diet, training and health problems? Could you afford the veterinary bills for your bitch's ante-natal care and for her litter? Do you know enough to help the bitch during her labour? Could you afford for your bitch to have a caesarean if she needs one? Am I equipped to raise the puppies with everything they need including worming, vaccinations, and socialisation? Most importantly of all perhaps, will you be able to place your pups into good homes and would you have the resources to take puppies back if the homes you sold them to prove unsuitable?

You should also remember that if all the puppies die, you will have no puppies to sell to offset the costs of the operation and after-care, so you will be seriously out of pocket. The very worst thing that could happen is for your bitch to die, which could leave you to rear any orphan puppies that remain.

Many people breed from their Border Terrier bitch because they would like to keep a puppy for themselves and most Border bitches sail through whelping and very much enjoy having puppies. You should not breed from your Border Terrier until at least the third time she comes in

season, at approximately eighteen months old, and ideally before she is three years old.

THE STUD DOG

The demands on dog breeders grow increasingly complex to ensure that future generations of dogs are bred responsibly. The over-riding consideration is the health of any potential puppies. This is particularly important when you are looking for a stud dog. He must have a good temperament, good health and maintain the breed type and characteristics of the Border Terrier. If your bitch came from a reputable breeder, go back to them and ask their advice about what stud dog to use. It is always best to use a proven, experienced stud dog. Predicting breed type and characteristics requires experience. If you are new to dog breeding then you should seriously consider joining an appropriate breed club where you will be able to meet and talk to some very experienced breeders.

You should certainly take the time to go and see the dog that may become the father of your puppies. You should also show your bitch's pedigree to the owner of the stud dog so that they can approve of her. Ask what the stud fee is and what conditions will be included; for example, do you get at least two matings if necessary and also, if your bitch fails to have puppies, does the stud fee cover a free return? Most stud dog owners offer this. You then need to work out when your bitch will be in season. You also need to work out when the puppies will be born.

There is a lot of time and work with puppies, so make sure you are going to be able to give it when they are born.

MATING

New breeders need to concentrate on finding out when their bitch comes into season. If you don't realise until your bitch has been in season for several days, it may be too late. This is disappointing if all the plans have been made. You will need to check your bitch virtually every day for the start of her season. The first sign is the vulva swelling. Some Border bitches' vulvas swell and do not show any signs of red discharge, others will show very little red discharge. Count from the day her vulva becomes swollen, just in case she is a bitch that has clear seasons.

Once your bitch is showing colour wait until the discharge becomes paler until you take her to be mated. You can check this by using either a white tissue to dab the vulva morning and night to determine the colour change, or you can put a white cover on her bedding so that you can monitor the colour change. If your bitch does not show any colour change you will need to count the days after she comes into season; ten to twelve days after coming in season is probably the best guide. However, some bitches are ready to mate after just six days into their season and have produced puppies from this mating, but this does not happen very often.

ABOVE: *Spend some time finding a suitable mate.*

Some maiden bitches, particularly pet bitches who are very humanised, can be reluctant to be mated even though they are in full season. This is why it is best to use an experienced stud dog who will not be put off by the bitch trying to ward him off. Alternatively, some maiden bitches will throw themselves at the dog, which makes it much better for everyone concerned. This amorous kind of bitch must be watched all the time while she is in season or she will find her own mate.

Once the bitch has been mated, you must keep her away from other male dogs until she is completely out of season. It would probably wise to keep her away from any male dog all the time she is in season

First-time breeders can also be nervous. Not everyone is aware that mating dogs "tie" or "lock" together during mating, on average usually for about twenty to thirty minutes. Sometimes dogs are locked together for hours, although this is very rare. It is usual to have your bitch mated twice, approximately forty-eight hours apart; once this is done, take your bitch home and keep her secure and quiet.

Occasionally a bitch will, after being mated, have a red discharge from her vulva, even as late as three to four weeks after mating. This usually indicates that the bitch is in whelp and there is activity within the womb. In the early days of pregnancy nothing should be changed, so treat her normally.

61

PREGNANCY

A bitch is usually pregnant for sixty-three days or nine weeks, but you should be prepared for her to give birth up to five days early or four days late.

You may be able to see that your bitch is pregnant from about three weeks, although some bitches do not show until seven weeks. Early signs of pregnancy are when her teats become pink or purple. she may also lose her appetite, and she may be sick. She may also become very quiet. On the other hand, she may show no signs at all but still could be pregnant. If you can see signs of her pregnancy very early, this may indicate that she is having a large litter. You should usually know whether she is in whelp or not by around six weeks.

As soon as you know that your bitch is pregnant, you need to change her diet from approximately five weeks onwards. As the puppies grow bigger, she will not be able to eat as much as she needs in just one feed. It is advisable to split her food into at least two meals a day, and up to four feeds a day towards the end of her pregnancy. It is very important to keep your bitch well nourished so that she will have the energy she needs to give birth. In the final two weeks, your bitch's exercise should be supervised so she is not overtired. Gentle exercise is good for her but car journeys should probably be avoided.

You should also make sure that your bitch's coat is kept well nourished. If it is in the winter months and she has a full coat it would be a good idea to strip her when she is about six weeks in whelp. If she needs to have a heated lamp over her and the puppies, she will find it too hot to lie with the pups if she has a full coat on. She will then leave the whelping box, which is not good for the pups. You should also

---

BIRTHING PARTNER

Your Border bitch may need a lot of reassurance and comforting during her labour. Equally, she may prefer to be alone. You can't be sure which way she will react until her labour actually starts.

remove the hair around her vulva to keep everything as clean as possible. Towards the end of the pregnancy, your bitch will probably have a sticky clear discharge from her vulva; this is normal. Any other colour is not and may mean she could be aborting her puppies and needs to see the vet.

WHELPING

As your bitch's due date approaches, you should decide where she will give birth. This needs to be somewhere comfortable and quiet. It would be sensible to inform your veterinary practice that your bitch is due to whelp, then, if you do need to consult them in the middle of the night, they are better able to give you any help you

ABOVE: *When Border puppies are first born, they spend their time eating and sleeping.*

need.

When your bitch goes into labour the best thing to do is to sit quietly near her and give her comfort and reassurance as and when she needs it. This stage of labour can last as long as twenty-four hours, and she may pant and tremble and dig up her bedding

ABOVE: *Border bitches generally make wonderful mothers.*

and look totally distressed. Don't worry, this is quite normal. You should only offer her clean water at this stage, as many bitches vomit during during labour. Your bitch will then go into the next stage when strong contractions will start. She will start to push as they increase in intensity. Her first pushes will be light and get much stronger. Your bitch may also pass a water bag which will then break, producing a clear liquid. Soon after this the contractions will get stronger and a puppy should be born within 20-30 minutes. This second stage of labour can last between 3 and 24 hours with puppies being born within 20 minutes of each other, but

there can be up to two hours between puppies. Mum will usually clean the puppy and bite through the umbilical cord. Some puppies are born tail first, but this isn't a problem.

If your bitch is busy delivering the next puppy, you should remove the membrane from the puppy and dry him with a clean facecloth. Rubbing will encourage him to take his first breathe and crying helps to clear his airways. You should also tie a piece of heavy thread around the cord approximately one inch from the pup's body, then tie another knot a little further from the first and use clean scissors to cut the cord between the knots. Be very careful not to cut too close to the puppy, and dip the end of the cord in tincture of iodine or chlorhexidine.

The third stage of labour is the passing of the placentas. You should

BELOW: *The newly-whelped bitch and puppies need comfort, warmth, peace and quiet.*

count them to make sure that none are retained in the uterus. Some bitches eat the placentas which contain nutrients that help her body to recover.

If you are unsure how things are going, the bitch is straining, or a placenta is retained, you should call your vet immediately.

When your bitch's labour is finished, you should get the mother something to eat and drink, and help her to go outside and relieve herself. You should remove and replace the soiled nest covers and then give the new family some time alone. Your bitch will probably want to sleep while she suckles the puppies. This first milk is very important as it contains colostrum

that contains the mother's antibodies and will protect them until they are old enough to be vaccinated. It may be wise for your vet to see the bitch and puppies soon after whelping. He will probably give the bitch an injection to ensure that any pieces of retained placenta are expelled. You should also get the puppies examined for any abnormalities.

AFTER THE WHELPING

If your bitch isn't interested in taking care of her puppies and doesn't show any concern for them for more than an hour you may need to take over looking after them. You should also consult your vet for advice. Hand-

ABOVE: *The newly-whelped bitch will need to eat well to produce milk for the puppies but might need tempting at first.*

rearing may be necessary especially if the bitch doesn't seem able to produce any milk. Other bitches are fantastic mothers and don't even want to leave their puppies so that they can go to the toilet.

It is very important that your new mother eats well. After eating the rich afterbirths your bitch may refuse food for a while and may go off her food altogether. You need to tempt her with some tasty treats and you will know what your bitch likes. This may be fillet steak or a dry biscuit. Once she has taken something, most bitches will continue to eat normally. Some bitches are ravenous when they have given birth. A large litter will not have left enough room in her stomach for her to take large meals and she may need to catch up. It is often preferable

to feed your bitch several small meals a day, consisting of really good quality food. She will also need to eat well to produce enough milk for her growing puppies.

WEANING THE PUPPIES

You should start weaning the puppies between the age of two and three weeks. Worming is also one of the most important things at this time. All puppies are born infected by worms and worms will prevent them from thriving. The puppies will need worming at two weeks of age. This can be done with a liquid puppy wormer that your vet will supply. They should be wormed twice more before the age of eight weeks. As you start to wean your puppies, you can give them saucers of warmed puppy milk several times a day. When the puppies have accepted the puppy milk, you can then move on to solids. This could be canned puppy meat, or dried food formulated for puppies. This should be fed warm. Dried food should be soaked until the puppies' teeth are stronger when It can be fed dry. Your puppies should also have constant access to fresh water. This is particularly important if you are feeding dried food as this can make the puppies very thirsty.

By the age of eight weeks, your

LEFT: *Keeping your new puppies' nails short will stop them scratching their mother.*

ABOVE: *These three-week-old puppies have started eating solid food.*

puppies should be fully weaned and eating and drinking independently. They will then be ready for re-homing.

ECLAMPSIA/MILK FEVER

Border mothers are prone to eclampsia, though most develop only a mild form of the illness. In any case, your bitch will need to see the vet.

This is a life-threatening condition that results from the bitch's loss of calcium during pregnancy (making the puppy's bones) and in her milk. It usually happens within a few weeks of her giving birth. Small dogs with large litters have an especially high risk of

the condition. It can be avoided by a good diet in pregnancy. Symptoms of this frightening illness (which can start very quickly) include panting, drooling, vomiting, restlessness, muscle spasms, convulsions, breathing difficulties, heart problems, and seizures. Eclampsia is a medical emergency and your dog will need urgent treatment, which will usually include calcium. This can be given intravenously. Once treated, your bitch should make a full and speedy recovery. However, the puppies should be fed for at least 24 or 36 hours. If there is any recurrence, she should not suckle the puppies again.

7 HEALTH CARE

It is very important that you register with a good vet either before your get your Border puppy, or very shortly afterwards. Recommendations from other local dog owners may help you. You should also make sure that you keep the vet's contact details and their out-of-hours arrangements for emergencies. One of the best things about Border Terriers is that, if they are well-looked-after, they are usually extremely healthy dogs. Hopefully, your visits to your vet will only be annually for the necessary booster vaccination, worming and, parasite remedies.

It is a very good to take your new puppy to the vet you have chosen and let the vet check him over as soon as possible. This will pick up any potential problems as early as possible. The vet will give the puppy a thorough physical examination, checking his eyes, ears, teeth, skin (for dry skin, fleas, and ticks), his tummy (for pain, enlarged organs, or any other abnormalities), his tummy button (for an umbilical hernia), his heart and lungs (with a stethoscope), his joints and knee caps (for normal movement), and his genitals.

Make sure that you are happy with how the vet handles your dog. If you have any concerns, find another vet that you feel more comfortable with.

RECOGNISING ILLNESS

Most Borders live healthy happy lives, but understanding how his body works will help you to recognize any problems sooner rather than later. Occasionally, your dog may be a little unwell and refuse his food. If this is the case, the best thing is to offer no further food for 24 hours. However, you should make sure that your dog always has free access to clean, fresh water. This is critical, as if a dog who is already unwell becomes dehydrated, this can lead to very serious illness. Most dogs will return to normal in the twenty-four hour period and will be happy to take their food.

ABOVE: *Choose a vet who makes your visit stress-free and handles your dog sensitively.*

ABOVE: *There have also been cases of Progressive Retinal Atrophy reported from America.*

Other symptoms that should mean an immediate trip to the vet include excessive water drinking, finding vomit containing blood, or continuous diarrhoea.

HEREDITARY DISEASES

Unlike many other modern breeds, the Border Terrier does not seem to be afflicted by any of the common inherited diseases. Only isolated cases of hereditary diseases have been reported by veterinarians. These include heart murmurs, hip dysplasia, Legg- Perthes disease, patella luxation, epilepsy and cataracts. In America, a few cases of Progressive Retinal

Atrophy have also been reported. Animals with these illnesses should not be bred from.

In the UK, there is an on-going investigation into Canine Epileptoid Cramping Syndrome (CECS) which particularly affects Border Terriers. This is a recently recognized disease whose symptoms include dizziness, trembling, muscle contractions, falling over, and stomach pain. The illness is usually controlled by diet, but this needs to be done under veterinary advice.

Another occasional Border abnormality is a kinked or bent tail. Although puppies are usually born with them; some will improve while others get worse. As a pet this condition won't matter much, but if you wish to show your Border it will be a problem.

COMMON AILMENTS

Anal glands Dogs have a pair of small sacs on either side of their anus. These anal glands produce a smelly, yellowish-gray to brownish pasty material, which is usually expelled when he defecates. Anal gland problems happen when the sacs become inflamed, impacted, infected, irritated, abscessed or affected by tumours. Dogs with anal sac problems can't properly eliminate the material that their glands normally produce. This causes lots of itchiness, pain and general discomfort. Unfortunately, anal sac problems are fairly common in domestic dogs. The reasons for this is not fully understood,

but several factors have been suggested, including obesity, bouts of diarrhoea, poor anal muscle tone, excessively faeces and excessive or retained anal glandular secretions.
Arthritis affects some older Border Terriers. The problem refers to the inflammation of one or more joints. It can be caused by traumatic injuries, physical deformities, joint infections, genetic predispositions, or problems with the immune system. Arthritis is painful, progressive and usually permanent. It is can lead to joint deformities, lameness, stiffness and loss of normal joint function. There are a number of things that owners can do to help their arthritic dogs lead full and fairly pain-free lives. These include weight management, dietary and lifestyle changes, surgical procedures and medications and supplements that provide pain relief. These treatments may also delay further joint damage.
Burns and scalds If your Border has the misfortune to be burned or scalded, he will need very similar treatment to a human patient. Put the burn under running cold water until the heat is gone. You may need to cut away some fur. Burn cream may be sufficient to heal a small burn, but a seriously burned dog should be taken to the vet immediately, as he may be suffering from potentially fatal shock.
Canker Your Border relies heavily on his hearing and will be very much upset by any ear problems. A dog's ears can

ABOVE: *To keep your dog healthy keep a check on his weight.*

become irritated for many reasons. Parasites can cause unbearable ear irritation. Fleas and mange mites can often settle in ears, causing hair loss, itchiness and inflammation. They can also contribute to waxy build up in the ear canal. Foreign objects such as ticks, seeds, grass seeds other plant material can work their way down the outer ear canal and cause pain and inflammation. Weather extremes may also contribute to ear problems. Moisture and heat create a rich habitat for bacterial proliferation, and icy weather can cause frostbite. Allergies are also often associated with ear discomfort. Reactions can be caused by food, particles, or parasites, especially fleas. Ear infections are caused by yeasts and bacteria and outer ear infections can move into the middle and inner ear. Whatever the problem, it is important to sort this out as secondary ear problems can develop if the underlying cause is not addressed.

Car-sickness Most Border Terriers don't suffer from car sickness as adult dogs, but puppies are sometimes sick in the car.

The best way to deal with car sickness is to prevent it. A number of conditioning techniques can be used to desensitize dogs to travelling in the car. But there are also effective medications to treat car sickness in dogs. The best are antihistamines and anti-nausea drugs. Antihistamines are most effective where the motion sickness seems to be caused by anxiety and the fear of travel. They calm the dog effectively and have few side effects. Anti-nausea medications are used when the car sickness is the result of the physical motion itself. Many of these car sick dogs love to travel, but can't handle the movement of the vehicle. Anti-nausea drugs are longer lasting than antihistamines, and may cause more serious side effects, such as confusion and even aggression. But most dogs become acclimatized to car travel within a short period of time, especially if they are conditioned to it slowly but regularly. Most Borders love going on car journeys with their owners once they begin to associate travel with pleasure.

Constipation often reflects dietary problems but affects many dogs from time-to-time. Symptoms of constipation can include non-productive straining, hard and dry motions, mucus from the anus, pain, soreness or swelling in the anal area, scooting, lack of appetite, abdominal bloating or discomfort, vomiting, weight loss, depression, and lethargy. While mild constipation usually resolves itself, severe constipation can be a medical emergency and should be treated very quickly. Middle-aged and older dogs tend to be more prone to constipation, as normal bowel activity tends to decrease with age. Dogs that do not drink enough water also tend to become constipated. Constipation is sometimes treated with laxatives to draw water into the intestines and soften the faeces. Enemas can also be used to evacuate the bowel. Another potential treatment option is adding milk to the dog's diet. The lactose in milk is difficult for dogs to digest and often causes diarrhoea. Olive or mineral oils are also used. If the attack goes on for longer than a day, you should contact your vet as your dog may have some kind of blockage. Borders do have a tendency to swallow toys, stones, and balls.

Diarrhoea is usually a symptom of some underlying medical condition rather than an illness in itself, but it requires prompt attention and treatment. It is usually acute (it comes and quickly and then goes away) but can be chronic (it comes on slowly and lasts for a long time). Unless the underlying cause is diagnosed and resolved, this unpleasant condition can keep coming and going. Unfortunately, there are dozens of diseases, disorders, substances and conditions that can cause diarrhoea. These can include dietary indiscretions, abrupt changes in diet, metabolic diseases (e.g. kidney problems, pancreatitis), poisons, prescribed drugs, a physical obstruction in the intestine, a viral infection, a bacterial infection, extreme stress, fungal infection, worm infestation, topical parasites, food allergies, cancer, ulcers, polyps, and

internal parasites. To avoid diarrhoea, owners should feed their Border with a high quality diet and try to prevent their dogs eating rubbish, contaminated foods, or non-edible items (such as plastic or balls). You should check your dog closely when he has diarrhoea. You should give him a solution of glucose and water to drink to make sure that he doesn't dehydrate. Fast him for 24 hours and then start to feed him with an easy-to-digest diet, chicken, or fish. If he doesn't improve quite quickly, you should take him to your vet.

Dog fights can cause horrible injuries and you will want to prevent this at any cost, but do not put yourself at risk. The most important priority it to separate the dogs without any further injuries to dogs or humans. Avoid getting hold of either dog by the collar as this is a good way to get bitten. A good way to shock dogs into separating is to throw a bucket of water over them. If this isn't possible, try to separate the dogs with something, a piece of cardboard or a brush for example. Once the dogs have been separated, keep them apart. You will need to see if there are any injuries. Wounds should be washed with warm antiseptic water, but dog bites will almost always be infected and your dog will need antibiotics.

Larger wounds may need stitching. These should be dressed and kept as clean as possible until your Border can be examined by a vet.

Fits and seizures can occur in dogs of any age, sex or breed. Luckily, Borders do not seem particularly prone to them although some other terriers are. In young dogs, most dog fits are epileptic seizures, seizures caused by toxins, metabolic disorders or conformational abnormalities. In older dogs seizures are sometimes caused by brain tumours. Puppies infested with worms can also fit, or if they have a reaction to their vaccinations. Your vet can correct this. It can be very distressing to see your dog having a fit. Most fits will be preceded by a pattern of altered behaviour. This may include staring into space, agitation, nervousness, restlessness, vocalization, clinginess, seeking seclusion, or confusion. The fit itself may cause the dog to show some of the following symptoms: weakness, loss of awareness, trembling, rigidity, stopping breathing

(for between 5 and 30 seconds), muscle twitching (especially in the face), chewing, frenzied bard, snapping, temporary blindness, vomiting, drooling, urination/defecation, collapse, or loss of consciousness. During the fit, you should not interfere, but make sure that your dog does not hurt himself. Once the fit is over, the dog will probably feel weak, wobbly and confused. Put him somewhere darkened and quiet where he can rest and recover. This might take around an hour. If your dog has another fit you should definitely take him to your vet. If he diagnoses epilepsy, there are veterinary drugs to control this.

Heatstroke is an elevation of a dog's core body temperature to intolerable levels. It is usually due to external factors (such as a dog being left in a hot car). The normal body temperature of dogs is between 100 and 102 degrees. Dogs don't tolerate high temperatures at all well because they don't sweat. Dogs dissipate body heat by panting, which helps them bring in cooler air from the outside, but when the external temperature is higher than a dog's body temperature, panting can't cool it down. Dogs with heat stroke become increasingly restless and uncomfortable as their temperature rises. They pant, have trouble breathing and become weak. Eventually, they lie down and slip into a coma. By this point, death is imminent unless the dog receives immediate aggressive medical attention. This could include soaking the dog with cool water until his temperature returns to normal. Unfortunately, many owners don't notice the signs of heat stroke until it is too late. Border Terriers easily fall victim to heatstroke, because their double coat insulates their bodies so well. Blue and tan Borders absorb the heat even more easily, so you need to take extra care if your dog is this colour.

Lameness is another of those canine conditions that can occur for a whole range of reasons. Dogs can go lame for many reasons. The most common causes are found in the foot itself so you should check this first for cuts, cracks, dried mud between the pads, thistles or swelling. Check the nails have not been damaged or that the nailbed is not infected. Sores between the pads can also cause lameness. If you find a foreign body in the paw, remove it and clean the foot with warm antiseptic water. In puppies, lameness can be caused by growing pains in the long bones.

If you can't find anything wrong with your dog's paw, feel further up his leg for any lumps or cuts. A good tip is to check both of his front or back legs to make sure that they are symmetrical. You can also feel if there is any unusual heat in the affected leg, especially around the joints. Again, see if both front or back legs feel the same temperature. Many cases of lameness

resolve themselves if your dog has a good rest overnight, but any lameness that remains unimproved for more than two days needs to be seen by the vet.

PARASITES – EXTERNAL

Fleas are small, flat, wingless, blood-sucking insects that are an irritation to dogs and their owners alike. They can also can carry and transmit serious diseases and other parasites (such as tapeworms). They are also the leading cause of skin problems in domestic dogs. Although they can't fly, fleas have powerful rear legs and can jump to extraordinary lengths. There are many types of fleas, all of which reproduce rapidly and profusely. Despite its name, the ordinary cat flea is by far the most common flea that bothers pet dogs. Dogs become infested if good flea prevention isn't followed. Dogs can also get fleas by having contact with other animals that have a flea problem. Fortunately, there are many things that dog owners can do to keep fleas under control. Most dogs that have fleas will

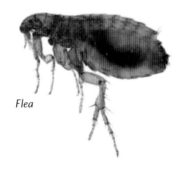

Flea

find them irritating and will scratch, but some can have a severe reaction to flea bites (flea dermatitis). If you think that you have found flea debris in your dog's coat, collect some of the black grit from the coat and put it on a white tissue. If the black grit goes blood-coloured when you dampen it, your dog has fleas.

Ticks are tiny parasites that feed on the blood of their hosts. They are usually found in sheep and cattle but can also affect domestic dogs in the summer months. Ticks are closely related to mites, spiders and scorpions. Ticks are attracted to animals by warmth, physical contact, and smell. They can carry and transmit bacterial organisms that cause infectious diseases - such as the bacteria that cause Lymes disease. Ticks crawl over the dog's body and find a suitable place to bite into the skin. It will stay in position for about two weeks until fully engorged with blood. At this stage, it will be about the size of a pea and beige in colour. Its bits cause irritation to the skin around the area of the bite, itchiness, head-shaking (if the tick is on the face or in the ears) and sometimes even paralysis. They also can cause a dog to suffer fever, appetite loss, pain, lethargy and depression. Ticks can be removed by using flea-control remedies that are also designed to remove ticks. Other methods involve removing the tick with special forceps, making sure you grasp the head. But if you don't manage to remove the tick's mouth parts, the bite can become infected.

Lice are small insects, averaging between 1.5 to 4 millimeters in length. Usually, they can be seen by the naked eye. They live for about four weeks. Their eggs (nits) can look like scurf on a dog's coat. They can be either biting or sucking lice. Lice are uncommon in clean, healthy, well-fed and well-maintained companion dogs and tend to thrive mostly on debilitated dogs that are old, run-down, malnourished or poorly cared for.

Harvest mites can infest dogs in the late summer and cause them to itch. Harvest Mites fee on warm blooded animals, swarming as an infestation. They're only a problem during this stage but can cause considerable discomfort to your dog and can be recognised as red dust clinging to your dog's hair. Harvest Mites are usually found in long grass, bushes, and plants and are most active during the day in dry and sunny conditions. Most flea treatments will also kill harvest mites.

PARASITES – INTERNAL

Roundworms are the most common internal parasites of dogs. Most puppies have some roundworm infection. Adult roundworms spend most of their lives in the dog's stomach and small intestine. Females lay hundreds of thousands of eggs daily, which pass in their stool and survive for years in the environment. Dogs become infected when they swallow roundworm eggs or eat infected rodents. Roundworms can cause stomach ache, vomiting, diarrhoea, and coughing. Infected dogs develop a dull coat, distended abdomen and stunted growth. Owners who notice one or more of these symptoms should go to the vet as quickly as possible. Dogs should be regularly wormed to control this problem.

Tapeworms are parasites that live inside a dog's small intestine. They can range from less than one inch to several feet in length. They are transmitted by fleas and lice. Tapeworms bury into the sensitive lining of a dog's intestine, feeding on blood and sucking up essential nutrients slowly and steadily over a long period of time. Adult tapeworms develop egg packets, which eventually break off and are passed out in the dog's faeces. Owners may see tapeworm segments crawling around their dog's rear end. They look like grains of rice. Modern tapeworm treatments are very effective and your vet will advise on how often you should

treat your dog.

Phantom pregnancy Border Terrier bitches seem particularly vulnerable to phantom pregnancies. It usually occurs somewhere between 6 and 12 weeks after a bitch goes through her normal heat cycle and is caused by an exaggerated response to normal hormonal changes, including elevated levels of the hormone progesterone. During this time, females can develop many of the signs of pregnancy, even if they aren't pregnant and haven't even been bred. Signs of false pregnancies include restlessness, whining, depression, anxiety and aggression. Many bitches engage in maternal behaviour, such as digging, nesting and mothering of stuffed toys, and some actually produce milk. These signs can be so convincing that even experienced breeders are fooled. Fortunately, with the help of modern technology, false

pregnancies are easy to diagnosis. They usually don't require treatment and go away on their own.

Phantom (or false) pregnancies can be completely avoided by having your bitch spayed.

Pyometra is a very serious uterine infection that usually occurs in bitches about six to eight weeks after their season has finished. It is an accumulation of puss insider the uterus, stemming from a bacterial infection. An affected bitch will develop an excessive thirst and may be sick. The discharge from her vulva will be an abnormal colour, yellow, green or red and thick. Pyometra can be life-threatening and must be treated as an emergency. It is uncommon, but still possible, that signs of false pregnancy will appear in a bitch who actually became pregnant and then either aborted or reabsorbed her puppies, in which case the risk of developing pyometra increases dramatically. Life-saving surgery may be needed to remove the ovaries and womb. In mild cases drugs may resolve the problem.

Shock. Anaphylactic shock is a serious allergic reaction to a substance that a dog has come into contact with. It is a complicated clinical syndrome that results in an inadequate blood supply to vital organs. If shock is not treated very quickly, the condition can be fatal. Many things can cause anaphylaxis in dogs. These include drugs, insecticides, bites, stings, antibiotics, anaesthetics,

mould, pollen, and some foodstuffs. An anaphylactic reaction usually happens suddenly within moments of the dog being exposed to the allergen. It may be a seizure, collapse, coma, or death. The dog's skin (especially his ears) will feel cold, his gums will be pale, and he will have a rapid heartbeat and breathing. Dogs with these symptoms should be taken to the vet as quickly as possible, and should be kept as warm as possible on their way there. If unconscious, keep the tongue out of the airway. In most cases a vet will treat anaphylactic shock with an intravenous catheter, using fluids to restore the dog's blood volume.

Shock can also follow a road accident, burn or another traumatic event.

SKIN PROBLEMS

Acute Moist Dermatitis or hot spots are firm, thickened, circular, raised, warm, hairless and often ulcerated skin lesions that are caused by repetitive licking and chewing in response to irritation. These sores are very painful and can become infected and smelly. They most commonly develop on the front paws, lower hind legs, under the ear flaps, or on the bottom. Affected dogs typically have some sort of allergic or underlying skin condition. This might be an allergy, infestation by fleas, mites, ticks or other external parasites, fungal infection, impacted anal glands, neglected grooming or bacterial infection. Depending on the cause of the problem, the vet might use antibiotics, steroids, anti-inflammatorys, or antihistamines. Analgesic drugs can be used for pain relief.

Demodectic Mange is caused by the Demodex mite, but is often considered to be a stress-related condition. It is usually seen in puppies between three and nine months of age but can occur in older dogs. In mild cases, it is not itchy or painful, but the dog may have patchy hair loss that usually appears on one or only a few places on their body. But if a dog develops generalized demodicosis, with widespread hair loss and infected sores, they often do become itchy and painful. If this happens, they may scratch, chew or bite at their infected areas, causing self-trauma and sores (lesions) that can become secondarily contaminated and infected by bacterial or other microorganisms. Severely infected dogs will become depressed and their skin may become thick and greasy, with black pigmentation and an unpleasant smell.

Sarcoptic Mange or "canine scabies" is a non-seasonal, intensely itchy and highly contagious skin disease caused by a little, spider-like mite called Sarcoptes scabiei. These mites are transferred between dogs by close physical contact and can also be transferred on bedding, brushes, shoes, collars, leads, and bowls. They burrow into a dog's skin where they feed and reproduce, causing irritation,

inflammation, and extreme itchiness. This in turn causes scratching, licking, biting, chewing, skin redness, hair loss and sores. Secondary bacterial infections are common at the burrowing and feeding sites. The most common treatment for this infection is with a topical scabicidal medication that kills the mites.

Cheyletiella Mange is also known as "Walking dandruff." It is an extremely contagious skin disease caused by parasitic mites. The disease got its nick-name because the pale Cheyletiella parasites are fairly large as far as mites go and can be seen scurrying along a dog's skin or coat, resembling dandruff flakes. Healthy dogs get walking dandruff by direct contact with infected animals. The mites burrow into the dog's skin, causing irritation, inflammation, raised red bumps, skin sores, chewing, and mild to severe itchiness. Fortunately, the condition is becoming less common because flea-control products also kill Cheyletiella mites. Young dogs with heavy "dandruff" over their necks and backs should be suspected of being infested with Cheyletiella mites. The standard treatment is weekly bathing to remove the scales, followed by weekly treatments with insecticidal rinses for a period of at least 6 to 8 weeks.

Stings. Most dogs, including Borders, will snap at annoying bees and wasps. Inevitably, this means that dogs will get stung on the mouth and tongue. Dogs also stand on the insects and get stung in the feet. Try to pull out stings in the paws with tweezers and bathe the sting area with bicarbonate of soda. If your dog is stung in the mouth you should take him to the vet in case he has an allergic reaction or goes into shock.

Summary

Although the Border Terrier is very adaptable and fulfils many roles, essentially he remains a working terrier. This means that he will need a lot of stimulation and leadership to keep him positively focused.

Borders are game, affectionate and stubborn as well as comedians. They are photogenic, they are not good gardeners, they eat anything, they will go anywhere wherever and whenever you want to go and they will love you to bits. All that your Border will need from you will be support, to be taught good manners, and given plenty of healthy food and exercise. With any luck, he will be virtually maintenance-free.